Be with me,
It's c

Poems

by

Avril Chester

Gibson Publishing

First published in the UK by Gibson Publishing

Be with me, It's c

ISBN 9780-99326-056-8

A CIP catalogue record for this title is available from the British Library.

Thank you.

I couldn't have done any of this without you, my incredible and amazing parents,
You are my rock and a gigantic support who never cease to give me reassurance.
To my Brother - you inspire me every day,
And yes, we can now go on holiday.
To my unbelievable friends, Bridget and Stew, Sharon and Chris,
The laughter, tears and virtual hugs gave me immeasurable strength, a big thank you and a kiss.
To my dearest Dione and wonderful Jo,
You gave me courage and helped me grow.
Linda and Ann thank you for sharing your journey with me,
Your hints, tips and reassurances, helped set me free.
To the fabulous Goodwood girls, my awesome university friends, to my college buddy & wife,
Beautiful Beverley & Gavin, marvellous Godmother, Aunts, Uncles and Cousins in my life.
To Elizabeth & Adrian, Elaine & Ian, Molly & David, Henry, Ursula & Roger, Sue and all my sensational family friends,
For old work colleagues, Facebook mates, Church Prayers and all those flowers, cards and colouring pens.
Thank you to my mentor Jon and my confidant Simon for encouraging me to take this leap of faith & broaden,
To all those at Eastbourne District General Hospital, your kindness & support will never be forgotten.

Most importantly to you and your support network,
A big thank you, I wish you all the love and hugs available in the world.

@MeMyselfAndAve

Be with me,

It's c

Is a book containing poems and adaptations,

To accompany you with the big c

It's also for family and friends who wish to learn,

And offer more than a cup of tea

To encourage you all to write your feelings,

Scribbling notes, fears and dreams is key

Breast cancer sparks so many emotions,

This is for you and me.

At least 10% from every book sold will be donated to Breast Cancer Care

Registered charity in England and Wales 1017658 and Scotland SC038104

For your notes, inspirations, scribbles, sighs,
For your frustrations, tears, hopes and dreams.
Keep your written expression just for your eye,
Or share with others at @bewithmeitsc

There is something there, I swear.
Perhaps it's my imagination, or poor examination.
No matter how many times I feel, it's real.
Panic is setting in, deep within.
My guts are churning, heart burning.
Devastation and fear, domineer.

What am I to do? This is not the 'flu.
I can't possibly lift the phone, perhaps I should postpone?
This is the worst you could do,
Take courage, you must get through.

The appointment is made, be brave.
Let's hope it's my imagination, post examination.
The doctor starts to feel, big breaths it's real.
Panic is setting in, deep within.
My body is burning, heart yearning.
All consuming fear, domineers.

For your notes, inspirations, scribbles, sighs,
frustrations, tears, hopes and dreams

First I am squished and then I am turned
Swap your boobs round Ma'am and don't be concerned

The machine zaps around me and then it is done
Put your clothes on lovely and quickly run

It is off to the next gig, this time I'm cold
It is only gel girl, not slime or mould

I try not to move but the pauses make me nervous
We're assessing your lump Ms and the best service

I really don't like this one, really don't like it at all
We're here every step love, would you like a shawl?

Is the injection soon? I don't like this tube
Can you hear my voice flower, all done with your boob

So it's just a little needle eh? Is there much pain?
Only slight discomfort lady, let me explain

Do we have to have three? perhaps results fluctuate
We've finally finished the tests, now all we can do is wait.

For your notes, inspirations, scribbles, sighs, frustrations, tears, hopes and dreams

Shall I compare thee to a stormy day?
Thou art more still and breathless,
wrapped in an intense deafness
as you over shadow the sun's rays.

The wait for results approaches closer and closer.
Every fearful thunder scream
threatens to engross her.

And the lightening doeth strike
like the final bells.
Alleviate the pain.
Has change happened to her cells?

Shall I compare thee to a summer's day? (Sonnet 18)
William Shakespeare

For your notes, inspirations, scribbles, sighs, frustrations, tears, hopes and dreams

You may have written alert
vivid in red and size,
You may be looking with sorrow
but still, like dust, I'll rise.

Does my diagnosis upset you?
The fear upon us like gloom,
'Cause I will walk slightly different now
from the waiting room.

Just like my spirit and like my soul
along with all my pride,
Just like there will be more hellos
let me tell you, I'll still rise.

I will not be broken
I will live to soldier on.
This cancer will not beat me
'Cause I'll rise, I'll rise and live on.

Still I rise
Maya Angelou

For your notes, inspirations, scribbles, sighs, frustrations, tears, hopes and dreams

It's the day before the mastectomy when all through the house
Not a creature was stirring not even a mouse
The decorations are up bringing a festive glow
There will be lots of laughter and the hope of ho ho ho

As she got up to enjoy the day
A small pang of emotion will bring her to pray
Then she'll go about her life as if nothing will happen
Buy presents, write cards and finish the wrapping

The day will appear soon enough
Small adjustments will be made as easy as a puff
She'll come round on the bed all confused and tired
With a drain, a bandage and the success as desired

The following days will be a strain
The temporary loss of one arm will feel like a drain
Her new shape might look funny and a little bit odd
But the cancer will be gone so all will give the nod

And they'll gather round the Christmas table all merry with feelings high
Eating succulent turkey with no sign of a sigh
Father Christmas if you can hear me now
I look forward to my new self, can we just limit the ow.

Twas the night before Christmas
Clement Clarke Moore

For your notes, inspirations, scribbles, sighs, frustrations, tears, hopes and dreams

A drain to my side
A bandage so wide
Painkillers flowing
My body slowing
Reliant on others
Even for the covers
I let out a sigh
And I cry
Is it really done?
My chest weighs a ton
We talk of cancer
But I cannot answer
My movement is restricted
This is not self-inflicted
Frustrations reign
This is insane
Can you pass me the water?
I feel like a toddler
I need the loo
Can you pass me the tissue?
I can't pull up my pants
Argh, I need a rant
All I can do is thank you
Deep breaths and don't overdo.

For your notes, inspirations, scribbles, sighs, frustrations, tears, hopes and dreams

Little Ms Patient
Had hesitation
When her compression plaster was taken away,
Along came Macmillan
Who banished the villain
Now Ms Patient enjoys a new day.

Little Miss Muffet
Unknown

For your notes, inspirations, scribbles, sighs, frustrations, tears, hopes and dreams

She has a hairy underarm
Not exactly a charm
She can't get to it with a razor
But you must continue to praise her

Emotions are a little wobbly
But she's tries some comedy
To make light of her hair
Rather than despair

So the deodorant is also off limits
Seriously lift her spirits
Hair and a different smell
Oh isn't this just swell

She stares a lot at her scar
She is a superstar
Despite her cording
Each arm movement is rewarding

She has a hairy underarm
She is so alarmed
Remind her she is precious
Still beautiful and vivacious.

For your notes, inspirations, scribbles, sighs,
frustrations, tears, hopes and dreams

Hey diddle diddle
Chant this riddle
Instead of watching TV,
Do your exercises
There are no compromises
No one else can do this
but me.

Hey diddle diddle
Unknown

For your notes, inspirations, scribbles, sighs, frustrations, tears, hopes and dreams

Roses are red
Violets are blue
Is there still beauty
When sliced from two?

Simply listen to your heart
Listen deep, listen hard…
You are still you
You will push through.

When the pain is all forgotten
Don't feel lost or broken
You are simply divine
And still my sweet valentine.

Roses are red
Gammer Gurton's Garland

For your notes, inspirations, scribbles, sighs, frustrations, tears, hopes and dreams

Maniga-boo
Mince-a-moo
Mena-filaicia-com

It's all gibberish to me
No, no I don't see
It's like you've hit me with a smoke bomb,

Receptor this, reoccurrence that
Grade, size and a margins chat,
Chemotherapy, Radiotherapy
Oh and Hormone Therapy
Is there a warranty with that?

Where are the ooh's and the ah's?
You've won a car, a holiday for two,
Perhaps a fridge freezer or cake mixer
I'd even take the cuddly toy or fondue,

Maniga-boo
Mince-a-moo
Mena-filaicia-com

It's all gibberish to me
No, no I don't want to see
Just leave me alone and carefree.

For your notes, inspirations, scribbles, sighs, frustrations, tears, hopes and dreams

Focus on a short term goal
Keep your mind occupied and in control,
Think of something you will do
Imagine feeling amazing in a day or two.

Remember this is not forever
This will eventually pass, however
There is not much I can immediately say
But focus on a short term goal each day.

Be alone or with a loved one
Stay in bed or on the settee until done,
You *must not* let it take your soul
Just try to focus on that short term goal.

For your notes, inspirations, scribbles, sighs, frustrations, tears, hopes and dreams

Waiting…

Tingling here
Tingling there
Is that a loose hair?

Waiting…

I gaze in the mirror
The change is nearer.
Is this the day I go bare?

Waiting…

I've been curious how it will happen
Anxious about my new fashion
I hope I feel beauty, not despair.

Oh, here we go
Should I take a photo?
I thought I was prepared.
Clumps start to come
I try not to be glum
But tears flow as I stare.
The patches are distressing
Come on, stop stressing
You can do bald with flair.
I suppose it's a big relief
Because I have the belief
My system reboot is getting there.

Now I can't forget it's c
So please, be with me.
I need your tender love and care.

For your notes, inspirations, scribbles, sighs, frustrations, tears, hopes and dreams

If you can remember the memories
If you can let go and trust,
If you can try to visualise
With all your must,
If you can endure the sickness
If you can face the pain,
If you can weather these physical changes
In this bumpy terrain,
There is a beautiful finish
If you can focus and believe,
The next trip and adventure
Is just there, you're on the eve.

If
Rudyard Kipling

For your notes, inspirations, scribbles, sighs, frustrations, tears, hopes and dreams

You! You! burning bright
dazzling like the stars at night,
Give a big yip and a hip-hip hooray
shine and dance like on Broadway.

The tablets will be your companion
side effects vast like a canyon,
But you are free, free to live
so panic not, be proud and jig.

Remember all those dreams you had
Go… go make them real,
Re-read your notes from here
Every scribble's a big deal.

The Tyger
William Blake

For your notes, inspirations, scribbles, sighs, frustrations, tears, hopes and dreams

To reconstruct, or not to reconstruct, that is the question:
Whether 'tis best personally to stay as you are
Or go under the knife just once more – to sleep,
No more; I cry, I cannot go on
But I can, so I will, once more – to sleep;
I love my prosthesis
It gives me a shape where there is none,
I simply find it awkward,
Sweaty and continues to rub me as time goes on;
But I've bought new swimwear
It hasn't been cheap,
If you can cope with your reflection
Then don't go – to sleep.

Hamlet Act 3, scene 1
William Shakespeare

This is for you to repeat and write in your own

I am…

I am bold
I am brave
I am bursting with life

I am dazzling
I am dignified
I am defiant in life

I am exquisite
I am enchanting
I am excited about life

I am foxy
I am fabulous
I am fun in life

I am gorgeous
I am glorious
I am grateful for life

I am marvellous
I am magnificent
I am merry on life

I am sexy
I am stunning
I am spectacular in life

I am thrilled
I am thankful
I will be triumphant in life.